FIΣRCΣ

ORIGIN

Written by

Sylvie Séverine Utteriyn

Dedication

To me

&

To anyone else whose vivid imagination never stops, cannot wait, won't rest and refuse to pause for one moment until they finally create what it is that they need to and must create to release out there into the world.

Book I

Katalina

SHE had a scar on her upper right shoulder blade.

Whenever she took a shower, she gently passed her fingers over it and felt the sensation of the pain that she had endured.

That pain stayed with her and tormented her mind as each day passed by.

That scar signified the memories of the affliction that she suffered from her past.

An injury that never healed and that will forever be in her future.

A shadow in her present.

That scar was the origin to how her story began.

And maybe one day she would tell her story.

But for now… her journey was defined by the actions that she took on her way to becoming FIERCE.

Men From The Past

SOMEWHERE DISTANT UNDER THE SUN: Katalina was home with her mom and dad when suddenly they heard commotion outside of their front door. There were women's voices shouting in Spanish to others nearby

"CORRE, CORRE, ellos vienen!"

"RUN, RUN, they're coming!"

Her dad knew who it was that those women were speaking of. Those men were looking for him and whoever else that he was hiding. And they will not hesitate to grab anyone else that was sheltered by the good people of this village.

In an instant, he walked to the mantlepiece to grab his rifle that was affixed on the wall above it. Next, he went to the kitchen and took a box out from underneath the sink. Inside of it, he had his Rambo knife and his Beretta M9 semi-automatic pistol. Katalina's dad was preparing himself to go out there to hold them off long enough so that his wife and daughter could escape safely.

He approached his wife and told her in Spanish that he loved her and that he will always love her "mi amor te llamo, te llamo siempre".

She began to cry because she knew deep down in her heart that this day would come.

He looked at his daughter and grabbed her small virgin hands and said to her that his heart wished that he did not have to leave them like this. But no matter what would happen, Esteban wanted his daughter to know that he was a brave man and that she was a fierce little girl with the strength of the spirits upon her "mi corazón desearía no tener que dejarte así. Pero se que te amo. Y pase lo que pase quiero que sepas que tu papi es valiente y que TU ères feroz. Ahora ve con los espíritus".

Katalina's mother tightly hugged her husband for one last time while uncontrollable tears rolled down her cheeks. She said to him in her mother tongue that she could not leave without him "mwen pa ka ale san ou"!

Her husband urged her to go quickly. He said to her to take Katalina away from here as far as she could.

He reassured her that he will find them wherever they are. But Katalina's mom did not want to go. She was willing to take the risk of being captured, if it meant that they would not have to be separated and stay together as a family.

But she had no choice.

Her husband needed to go out there to slow them down.

Esteban thought to himself that he needed to go outhere quickly so that his family had enough time to escape safely. They were all that he *had*. He could not let them capture Katalina and Helena. They gave him purpose and they made him a better man "... son todo lo que tengo.... y me hicieron un mejor hombre".

Katalina looked at her dad and started to cry asking him what was happening and why he was not coming with them "papa sak gen en pou ki sa ou pap vini avek nou"?

He replied to her that she should not worry her little heart about it and that he needed to stay back for a short while to protect them. But they needed to leave their home now. And as soon as this was done he would rejoin them

"no te preocupes hija mía, lo haré pero después de hacer esto. Tengo que quedarme atrás para protegerte a ti y a tu madre".

"¡Debes ir ahora con tu madre!"

Katalina tried to hold her tears but she couldn't because she knew that something was not right.

He rushed them both to leave at once and without any further delay.

Those men were approaching. He stepped out the front door while Katalina and her mother left using the back door and took nothing with them. All that they had were the clothes on their backs. Katalina turnt back and took one more look at the only home that she ever knew.

Soon after their departure, Katalina heard yells and gunshots. She could tell that her dad was already fighting those men to hold them off from reaching their home.

Helena and Katalina managed to make a run for it. They witnessed violent scenes that took place as they fled. They ran into other neighbors that urged them to hurry and to get to the truck at the end of the road ahead if they were to all make it out of the village alive. Katalina begged her mom to wait for her dad.

But her mom said to her that they needed to go and that she was sure that her father would find them later "nou dwe ale pitit mwen, papa ou pral jwenn nou mwen séten de sa".

The other men on that truck would not have it to risk everyone else's life for one man. And so, the driver stepped on the gas and the truck took off in no time. As it pulled away, Katalina and her mother looked at the terrifying scene from afar. Her father was on his knees with a gun to his head. A grenade exploded and the smoke spread everywhere. That was the last thing that they saw. They did not know what happened next and they feared the worst.

Helena took her child and leaned her head on her bosom. She spoke to her in her native language and whispered to her that everything will be okay. She reminded Katalina of her father's words and she said to her to always "remember what your father taught you. Wherever that you go the spirits will be with you to protect you. And when you are afraid, call on them to give you vision, to shield you from harm and to give you the fearlessness of a tiger. You are your father's child. Always remember who you are, my daughter".

Helena traced the sign of the cross on her child's forehead. She gently closed Katalina's eyes with her fingers and held on to her firmly as to never let her go.

HOURS LATER: Everyone on the truck remained silent during the ride. Some children fell asleep tired from the whole event. Others were staring out aimlessly. Stopping along the way to get food was not on anyone's mind and it would be dangerous to do so.

However, two questions definitely preoccupied everyone's thought: would they reach their destination safely, wherever it was that they were going to? And what would their future hold once there?

Snatched

They had traveled on dirty, bumpy and narrow back roads to avoid detection. The sun had begun to set. That evening the sky was darker than usual. And the wind was light and quick on its feet. By now, everyone on that truck was just exhausted. At some point during the ride, they all looked at one another and saw the expression of uncertainty settling on each others' faces.

They were unaware of where they were going. But, as their minds wondered about what would come next, they were certain that they had been the only ones that had made it out of the village unhurt.

That was what they thought at least.

Suddenly, the truck came to a brusque halt and everyone froze in their position. The path ahead was blocked by armed men standing in the front and the back of pickup trucks and SUVs "camionetas y jeepetas".

Two out of those unknown men had motioned the driver to come to a full stop.

As the men walked toward the vehicle, there was a sense of panic in the driver's voice as he spoke to his comrade next to him seated in the passenger side. The driver noticed that these armed men were wearing military uniforms. They reached the driver's side door and as they stood there they told him to turn off his engine.

Without being solicited, the driver told them that they were coming from a long trip and that they were heading back home. But these men were not interested in his answer. They wanted to see the cargo of his truck. Not giving him any chance to reply any further, they forced them both to get out of the vehicle.

Meanwhile, since Katalina's mother had heard and understood in Spanish what was being said up front by *those men*, she went ahead and translated everything to the others that did not quite understand, unfortunately, what was about to happen next.

All four of them walked around to the back of the vehicle. They had the driver lift the soft top cabs of the truck.

Upon seeing *what* was inside, one of the armed men yelled out in Spanish to his other compadres that were up front to call *the boss* because they believed that they had found something of interest "llama al Jefe, tenemos algo aquí"!

In the meantime, those same armed men had everyone get off the truck. Most of the passengers were children and women with a few men.

A man looking to be *El Jefe* came to examine the *cargo* and with one nod of the head his men pointed their guns at the only other men there that could have resisted their commands and put up a fight.

El Jefe ordenó his men to take with them *all* of the *girls*.

"¡Llevar a las niñas!"

Katalina was snatched out of her mother's arms and so were the other young girls that were there too. The women all started to cry hysterically. The few men that had accompanied them thus far and that were part of the cargo tried to intervene. But, they were outnumbered by men with guns. It did not take long for El Jefe's men to carry away the girls and to put them onto the back of their vehicles.

And just like that, the girls disappeared into the night. As Katalina was forced to get in the back of those men's trucks the sound of her mother's screams echoed in her ears

"KATALINAA! Noooo, pitit MWEN"!

There was no one else in sight that could have helped them. The women were in shock. The driver of the truck and the other male passengers tried to convince the *mothers* that they needed to get back on the road. But, the women would not hear it. Instead, they blamed them for what had happened "how could you stand there and do NOTHING!...".

Gustavo, the driver, had heard stories before about *those men* that specifically looked to snatch *little girls* and sometimes women. But, he was an experienced driver. He knew all of the roads to take and not to take when transporting *human cargo*. This had never happened to him before. He momentarily blamed himself but quickly realized that there must be *a leak* into their underground operations. Gustavo let the thought rest in his mind for now. He needed to get his remaining passengers back onto his truck to drive them to their destination fast. Then, he would go back to the village for *Esteban.*

The Compound

SHORTLY AFTER: they arrived at the *compound*. All of the young girls were quickly put in a sort of a line up. Then, one by one they were photographed and cataloged.

The girls were surrounded by the R.I.D.S of the world. By men that looked and were ruthless, indignant, dangerous and sinful. The girls were shivering. Some were crying. Others panicked not knowing what to expect or what to do. As a natural reaction they aimed to run. But just like rabbits their attempt to hop away quickly got shut down effortlessly. All that Katalina and those girls had now was each other. Those men could see the looks of despair and fear into their eyes. Katalina felt like a prey and so did the other girls. Those predators were looking at them ready to snatch each one of them to eat as a meal that they would devour *sans pitié!*

With the approval of El Jefe, one by one some of the girls were taken away by his men to be prepped and ready to be delivered to *buyers*.

Katalina and Ezabella were to stay with him. He liked them young, with soft skin and clean fingernails.

Katalina soon learned that *He*, El Jefe, was a man with very few words.

That same night, Tito arrived late for duty at the compound. He did not even get a chance to reply to El

Jefe's question about why he was late when a bullet went straight through his head. El Jefe despised it when his own men made him wait. Jefe was known for his impulsiveness and trigger fingers. When it came down to doing business, El Jefe thought that to make someone wait was the ultimate disrespect and lack of consideration for one's precious time.

But this incident that had occurred in front of Katalina was not the only reason that El Jefe was also known for.

It seemed as though one of his so-called distinct skills was to inflict pain on pristine young girls; and, he took pleasure in it. The louder the young girls would scream the more he rejoiced. El Jefe knew exactly how to make their voices shriek. He knew exactly how to make them beg and cry relentlessly. That was his natural talent so he thought.

At times, he would tie his victims' hands and blindfold them to make their fear rise as they remained in suspense about what their fate was going to be next.

Once that he would begin his torture on his victim, the sound of her voice squealing with what was left of her strength as she could not take the pain anymore would bounce around the walls in that small, dark, hot and wet room.

His objective was to have those young girls heed to everything that they were told to do as exactly as they were told to do, whenever and with whomever. They were not to have any opinions, comments, questions or concerns about anything let alone say anything or to even refuse a direct order given. In his eyes, El Jefe thought that *training* them at such a young age would make for perfect wives and concubines to sell at a high price value to the highest bidder. But he would also auction off some of the girls to be part of some *experimentations* with whom he would call *the good doctor*. No one knew exactly what they were all about. And even if they did, they would be wise to keep that information to themselves. Being accused of spreading rumors at the compound will give El Jefe's men *carte blanche* to deal with that *offender* swiftly and accordingly. And that was just as bad as dealing with El Jefe himself. Only months later did Katalina find out that El Jefe was involved in much more than just *trafficking*.

He was infamously known as "El Jefe" to the well hidden underworld market of human trafficking.

El Jefe, surely, was a predator *now*. Yet, he never predicted that in some distant future, he was bound to be a hunted *prey*.

Unbearable First Weeks

The first few weeks at the compound felt like they were strictly dedicated to teach Katalina, Ezabella and the rest of the girls the every day routines until their time had arrived to be sent off.

All of the girls at the compound were in their teenage years. For the exception of the few women that were referred to as *madrès* who had been living at the compound for what had seemed to be an eternity. These women' role at the compound was to have these young girls learn and to follow El Jefe's draconian rules to the T while they were there in holding before being sold off.

For the young girls who appeared to have begun their menstrual cycle, El Jefe had them separated from those that did not. Next, they were shipped away as *properties of value* only to live a life of atrocities in different parts of the world. Or a life of bondage masqueraded as *marriage.* If no one in particular had shown a certain interest in any of them from the pool of El Jefe's *elite* clientèle.

It did not take long for Katalina and Ezabella to learn how awful and disgusting of a human being El Jefe was. Not a few days had passed and already, El Jefe would have Katalina and Ezabella be the source of his unartistic inspiration by ordering them both to watch him as he would perform sexual acts in front of them with women that he had paid for.

In his twisted mind, he thought that the girls needed to learn how to be *obedient women* and *this* was one way to do it. El Jefe would expose himself in front of Katalina and force her to watch his male genitalia and to deal with his indecent exposures all together. Katalina's sensitivity as a child was gone by the bluntness of his obscene acts. Her fragile soul could not take this horror as she was terrified and speechless. In her mind, all that she could think about in moments like these were the memories of her parents and all of the good people that she had once lived with back at her village.

The day to day life at the compound became more and more brutal for Katalina and Ezabella. One day Jefe had his guards fetch Katalina and Ezabella to be brought over to his room. After they entered, they stood by the door waiting for his directions. He gave them both a smile and looked on with favor.

El Jefe thought to himself that *they seemed to have adjusted well.*

Katalina began to feel very uncomfortable every time that she was in his presence. He noticed her uneasiness and constantly demanded that she come closer to him at once. Katalina always walked toward him as slowly as she could. Even a snail would have gone faster than her at this point. By doing so, in her mind, she hoped *if only he would change his mind.*

Nevertheless, El Jefe entertained her trivial attempt that day. He was seated at the tip of what looked like a makeshift bed that was all frame with a so-called mattress on top of it. That man had more than enough money to get himself a decent bed. However; his choice implied that the acts that he had performed on this provisional bed with the women that he had paid for did not necessitate for them to be comfortable because he had but little regard for them.

He asked to see Katalina's hands. She hesitated for a short moment. Then she stretched out her arms in front of her. As she did so, he grabbed them both and sharply pulled her toward him so that she could be in a kneeling position in front of him. As he looked at her, he spoke to her softly about trivial things while having her left hand travel up his leg to be set on his private part.

Katalina quickly pulled back.

She was shaken to her core.

He swiftly grabbed her hand again but this time, he held it firmly while placing it back to where it was. His soft voice and tender look had vanished.

Ezabella's eyes swelled up with tears. She watched on and was visibly enraged but did not seem to be shocked as if she had already been exposed to such a revolting act.

Nonetheless, they both felt repugnance by the actions of El Jefe who in no time had Katalina's hand move up and down in a steady motion.

As Katalina heard his moans intensifying, she closed her eyes to allow herself to be somewhere safe in her mind.

She reminisced about her childhood and how she missed her parents' love and her village. To her knowledge Katalina was her parents' only child. But for some strange reason at that moment, she wished she had brothers and sisters.

The Scar

At times, El Jefe would have Katalina and Ezabella help him bathe for no other reason than to be a pervert. He could have easily just ordered any of the madrès at the compound to *assist* him while he took his baths.

But he did not.

Instead, he had a particular interest in the duo from day one.

Katalina was desperate to find a way to escape from the compound after weeks of being there. She hadn't been in a good mood and she had lost her appetite.

One thing was for certain, all of the girls at the compound were well fed per El Jefe's wishes. There must have been a logical explanation behind his intention aforementioned. The meals were not five stars but food was plenty and readily available if any of the girls' body appearances gave an impression that they were malnourished. Katalina's small body frame had gotten noticed by one of the madrès: *Liliana.*

Katalina spent two weeks being coerced to eat. Every single day, madrè Liliana would bring her three meals to eat in that room where she had been held up, until she showed improvements with her condition. Madrè Liliana was not amicable. She was stern and did not tolerate little girls' tantrums about refusing to eat. As if that would have changed their present circumstance at the compound.

She would closely watch Katalina eat and even spoon fed her when she perceived any attempts to babysit each mouthful of food in her mouth.

Katalina had not seen Ezabella during this time and kept on wondering how she was doing? As much as Katalina hated it to be alone in that room, she did take advantage of the alone time that she was given without having to obey any of El Jefe's requests.

The time that she spent in isolation was a moment of reprieve from all of the punishments that Jefe would have handed down on the girls including herself for any little infractions.

But her time in that room would end soon.

And, it surely did.

Madrè Liliana came to the room one day early in the morning and told her that El Jefe wanted to see her. Apparently, Liliana had reported back rather sooner than later that Katalina had gained her weight back and that she was cleared to leave the *feeding room*. Katalina was dreading her exit because she knew that El Jefe would immediately ask to see her. And, he did. Katalina loathed madrè Liliana. She just could not understand how as a woman and perhaps as a mother she seemed to be fine with all of *this?*

Katalina was brought to him.

Upon seeing El Jefe's face, she felt a sense of blind rage rising inside of her. Therefore, she had not noticed that Ezabella was already there.

Jefe came out of the bath tub and walked toward her as she was leaning against the wall. She slid down to a sitting position in one of the corners of that so-called bathroom. While standing unrobbed in the middle of the room, he ordered her to walk to him at once. It was just the three of them alone in that bathroom. As always, Jefe's guards were not too far away outside of that door.

Katalina did not want to obey any commands that that man would order her to do. So she refused his first direction and the next one. Katalina herself did not know what possessed her at that moment to have reacted so boldly, knowing that there would be a severe consequence that would follow her disobedience.

El Jefe attempted to use that soft voice of his again.

He pretended to be patient to indicate to Katalina that he was okay with her refusal and that nothing would happen to her as long as she would listen to him next.

His face showed a sign of calmness. However, he displayed a fake smile to convince Katalina that nothing would happen to her.

Katalina's naïveté made her believe that after all El Jefe *may not be that upset with her.* But she had been fooled.

El Jefe dijo "ven Katalina. Ven ahora, está bien. No va a pasar nada". He was assuring her once again to come to him and that nothing would happen to her.

Ezabella froze and eyeballed Katalina. She gave her the look that said "please listen to him, you don't want to go to that room".

Persuaded by Jefe's soft facial expression and Ezabella's stare down, Katalina got up and walked toward him.

Jefe sure knew how to deceive these young girls *every* time. But of course he would know how to. He was an obnoxious and experienced man.

El Jefe fed off the gullibility of these young girls and that was one of the reasons why he adored them so much.

What happened next, Katalina was not ready for it.

Once close enough, at arm's length, El Jefe violently grabbed Katalina by her hair and threatened her that she would be sent to the punishment *box* for disobeying him if she did not do what he would ask of her next.

Katalina refused again.

El Jefe gave Katalina one last soft look. Then, with one gesture, he furiously struck her with the back of his hand across her face.

Ezabella let out a scream.

Katalina fell flat onto the ground hitting her head. Ezabella rushed to her side and called out her name several times.

"KATALINA, KATALINA, KATALINAAA!"

Ezabella was crying hysterically at the sight of blood coming from Katalina's mouth. It seemed as though El Jefe had knocked out one of her teeth. But he quickly told Ezabella to hush her mouth before she suffered the same consequence.

Katalina opened her eyes. She felt dizzy. Her sight was blurry, but she was somewhat conscious.

Jefe had barely dried his body and managed to put on his pants when the guards pushed open the door and rushed in to ask their boss what had happened "que paso, que paso Jefe "!

He ordered them to take Katalina away to the *box* at once. He told them to tie her hands and to leave her there because he will deal with her shortly.

"Atenle sus manos y déjala allí. Me ocuparé de ella en breve."

One guard roughly grabbed Katalina by her arm and raised her up to walk. The other one barely gave her a chance to stand steadily when he pushed the buttstock of his rifle gun onto her back to have her hurry up to walk.

Ezabella was terrified. She was escorted to her room and had no meal for the night. This was the first time that Ezabella had been denied a meal.

While in the room, Ezabella deep down thought to herself that it was not fair.... And why should she also be punished when all that she tried to do was to warn Katalina....

Ezabella quickly felt guilty for that selfish thought that crossed her mind. Katalina was like a sister to her and the only one that she had. She wanted to protect her. But, at that moment, Ezabella felt powerless.

She envisioned a future where her and Katalina would be free and away from *this place*.... She shook her head as a way to regain her determination to find a way out. So she forced herself to think about all possible ways that she could escape the compound with Katalina by her side.

Meanwhile, Katalina was in the dark hot room crying and afraid. Her hands were tied with a rope that had a knot that was hooked above her head that left her barely standing on her two feet.

She awaited her fate.

What would El Jefe do to her?

She did not know.

He arrived moments later and entered the room. He walked toward her slowly and observed her body shivering. He approached her and held her chin with his fingers and said to her with his hot breath that he was disappointed in her behavior "sabes Katalina, estoy decepcionado de ti".

He began to walk around her in a circle. Then, he stopped and stood right behind her back. Next, he put his hands around her waist and started to feel her up.

Katalina cried and breathlessly asked him to stop.

She begged him to end what he was doing to her.

With a soft voice he reassured her that he was not going to hurt her. But, she knew better now than to believe his lies.

She cried uncontrollably and pleaded with him that she won't disobey him ever again. He told her that he believed her and that he was sure that she wouldn't either. But Katalina knew that Jefe was not a man of his words.

Disobedience in his eyes was a sin.

He convinced himself that he was a *man of God.*

And as a man of God, even if Katalina was one of his *prize* possessions; El Jefe had to afflict upon her a punishment for her trespass against him.

He tightly placed his arms around her waist and smelled her hair down to her neck. He told her that he could smell the scent of fresh blood coming soon. He alluded to Katalina having her first menstrual cycle.

Then, in his mind, El Jefe had sickening thoughts of what he would do to Katalina in his bed once the time would come. He smirked at the idea that he *will soon have her all to himself.*

But for now he had to make her learn a lesson. He put his hand in his pants pocket and pulled out a pocket knife.

He unfolded it.

With his left arm, El Jefe firmly held on to Katalina's body by her waist and leaned all of his weight onto her to have her cease from moving.

He laid the tip of the knife on her cheek and told her to stop moving otherwise he would make her agony last longer.

Katalina trembled like a chicken ready to be executed at a slaughterhouse. El Jefe's grip was very tight. She was still shaking while the knife traveled from her cheek down to her shoulder blade where it rested. El Jefe applied pressure there and Katalina screamed at the top of her lungs.

Jefe didn't care for her screams; he loved it!

He managed to carve out something on Katalina's shoulder before she let out one last scream with all of her might that was so loud that she passed out afterward.

THE NEXT DAY: Katalina woke up to the sight of Ezabella in the room putting a wet cloth over her forehead that was burning hot. Katalina's fresh wound was still bleeding. The blood had gotten onto the bed flimsy cover sheets. The whole occurrence with El Jefe had left her in such a state that she had fallen ill.

Katalina stayed in bed for a couple of days. Madrè Liliana came to check on her and to make sure that Ezabella was tending to the wound well. The last thing that Liliana thought about before leaving the room was that El Jefe was a mere minded man, who over the years still did not gain any common sense about simple things. To madrè Liliana, El Jefe's impulsiveness was worse than that of small children who felt entitled to everything that they saw once they cried hard and loud enough for it "estúpido, que nunca estaba pensado este hombre"!

But Katalina and Ezabella would never know that *this* was how she felt and thought about him.

Liliana was *loyal.*

Despite her contempt for El Jefe, her allegiance was to him.

After what she had experienced in the punishment room at the hands of El Jefe, Katalina said no more.

Not one word came out of her mouth for a long time.

Even Ezabella could not get her to speak to her. The smallest spark of happiness that Katalina had managed to keep as a child had now faded away.

El Jefe would be proud to know that Katalina had definitely learned her *lesson.*

Ezabella tried to comfort her. And reminded her that one day, they will get out of here "te lo prometo".

Everything Else But That

They were sent away at the first sign of blood. This was one of the moments that El Jefe waited for to consummate marriage with the girls' future captors.

Ezabella was worried.

Before they had been kidnapped, Ezabella and Katalina had lived in the same village. But they had never spoken to each other. They were two strangers. They rarely would cross paths and when they did Ezabella's mom would always behave strangely. Ezabella's father had secretly arranged for her to be married ever since her birth. She did not know why since her parents were both in good health and had more than enough financially to care for her especially because she was their only child. So, in an attempt to delay the whole process after finding out what her husband had done, Ezabella's mom used to give her *concoctions.* They used to make Ezabella sick *but* simultaneously obstructed her menstrual cycle for a long time. That day when those men came into their village searching for Katalina's dad, Ezabella complained to her mom that she was tired of swallowing this *bitter tea* every day. Her mom paid her no mind because she knew the reasons behind her actions. All that Esperanza wanted for her daughter was to be free to choose her own path in life. Ezabella was her only child; therefore; she refused to concede to her husband's scheme for an arranged marriage for her daughter.

Ultimately, Esperanza knew that she would not be able to keep up at deceiving her husband any longer because he had become suspicious. Ezabella was getting older and yet she still had not begun to menstruate.

So on that day in question, Esperanza took advantage of the chaos that was happening in the village.

While her husband had stepped outside to get the car ready so that they could flee, she grabbed Ezabella's hand and foolishly ran out the front door with her to the end of the road where she had spotted some of the neighbors getting onto a truck.

Carlos came back momentarily to find an empty house.

His wife and child had vanished.

Ever since that day, Ezabella felt resentment for her mother. She still loved her; but she just could not forgive her mom's stupid and careless mistake that had led her here at the compound.

After the first few weeks there, Ezabella had started to feel cramps. She would manage her pain well enough so that no one would find out. But, deep down in her heart, she sure wished she had access to drink that bitter tea that her mother used to give her.

Ezabella was terrified at the thought of if anyone were to notice, it would not take long for the madrès to know that her first menstrual cycle would come soon. And that would mean that Ezabella would be sent away and would never see Katalina again.

The two had become sisters and relied on each other for everything, especially emotional support while remaining captives at the compound.

There was no way that Ezabella was going to let El Jefe separate them.

Ezabella was older than Katalina. And ever since the two had arrived at the compound, she felt a sense of duty toward her, like a big sister.

The time had come where she desperately needed to come up with an escape plan for her and Katalina.

By now, they had been at the compound for months already. But for both of them those months felt like forever. Ezabella had contemplated her escape ever since her arrival at the compound. It would be hard to plan for an escape when El Jefe constantly had her and Katalina by his side. Ezabella believed that she needed an ally but who could she trust beside Katalina? Nevertheless, she was determined to come up with a plan no matter what.

Fanaa-Anni

At the compound it was customary for El Jefe to wait for the first drop of blood to make a marriage *official.* His practice was absurd. El Jefe's business was not to marry *two consenting adults,* instead it was about making money and more money by kidnapping and taking advantage of vulnerable girls.

In the minds of Katalina and Ezabella, this so-called marriage was cruel eternal-bondage-. To subjugate young girls to be under the control of *beasts* that only cared about satisfying their darkest and most barbarous perverted sexual desires and whatever else their minds thought about....

For this, El Jefe was a wicked man for facilitating all of it. Regardless of whatever everyone else thought about the way that he made his money or and conducted his affairs, in his eyes, El Jefe considered himself a *respectable* businessman.

Obviously, the young and unaware bride- to-be was in no rush to see that day. They had no idea of what was awaiting them once that day would arrive. They did not even know that they were brides in the first place.

And how could they have known at such a young age?

Katalina was privy to having witnessed such an event one day while in the presence of El Jefe and his visitor that had come to the compound.

El Jefe was a *great host* to his guests.

He showed manners and the utmost politeness.

Katalina was shocked to see those characteristic traits from him. To her the way that she had known him to be, he did not seem to care about what people thought or said about him.

He showed confidence about himself so much that he did not have to play nice or pretend to be a *decent gentleman* for anyone.

Everyone that was part of his network already knew what kind of *monster* he really was. Nonetheless, as Katalina stood in the back of the room from where they were, she watched as he carried on his charade.

He grabbed two shot glasses.

He poured himself a drink and one for his guest too.

Then they both raised their glass in the air and as they clinked them, they shouted *Bastravia*! They cocked their heads back and threw the hot liquid down their throats one time.

For Katalina, it looked like that cheer was the result of both men being satisfied with *a deal* well done.

El Jefe then took the shot glass from the man's hand and just like that another separation happened.

Anni was gone, sold off.

Katalina could not understand how El Jefe could be so heartless.

That night, she told Ezabella that she could not get the picture out of her mind of Anni being taken away just like that. By some strange man that she never had seen before.

Katalina had nightmares for days about this.

Ezabella was not present when all of this had happened.

Instead El Jefe had ordered her to stay in her room. His guards were nearby to stand watch as always. And, of course, madrè Liliana was annoyingly checking on her every five seconds to make sure that she was still in that room.

It became clear to both of them that El Jefe showed Katalina *preferential attention*. But in a way, it worked out for Ezabella as she was actively occupied with putting together an escape plan.

All that she knew about the girl was that her name was Anni.

Ezabella tried to reassure Katalina that she had a plan and that they too would leave the compound but not to be in bondage. Instead, it would be to finally regain their freedom and to find their families that they had lost.

Katalina kept on wondering how El Jefe found all of those young girls that would come in and soon after be taken away so fast off the compound. Of course, he had kidnapped them just like he did for Ezabella and her but where were those girls from?

To Katalina, *this place* was like a revolving door. It was one thing to be taken away for the first time but suffering the same event a second time around was too much. Katalina could not see herself being transported to another place and another and the next.

She too was thinking about an escape plan.

But in the meantime, Katalina and Ezabella sadly thought that they were somewhat *lucky* to have caught the attention of El Jefe once they had arrived at the compound that day.

It was obvious to them, by now, that the compound was a sort of *hub* and definitely not a place where the girls that were brought in would stay there for long. Katalina and Ezabella could not suffer another transition to yet another strange place with an unknown devil. They had been kidnapped and forcefully brought to the compound and had not even begun to heal from this first horror. There was no way that Katalina and Ezabella would stand to be taken away again. The same way that they thought about escaping they wondered if any of the other girls had thought about it the same.

Katalina figured that maybe Anni too had planned an escape but just never got to act on it after her time was cut short.

Katalina just could not get Anni out of her mind.

DAYS LATER: Ezabella noticed that El Jefe was more demanding than usual. He lashed out at Katalina for not running his bath water quickly enough. Although it was not in his nature to be nice, it certainly was not like him to be irritated at small things such as this. Suddenly, his guards came knocking on the door and he got even angrier. They entered and told him that there was some bad news "malas noticias Jefe"!

The girl that was sent away was brought back.

The client stated that he was not happy with the *goods*.

That news made El Jefe furious.

He stormed out of the bathroom totally forgetting about Katalina and Ezabella who stood there.

When a girl was brought back to him as a *damaged good* or *unobedient* it was as if El Jefe's reputation was in jeopardy for not delivering on his promise.

Anni came back to the compound physically, psychologically and emotionally *injured*.

She went *mad*.

Anni roamed the compound and spent all of her time in and out of *lock out*. El Jefe did not want to part ways with her so easily.

He was enraged that Anni had been brought back to him. Because that meant that what he was *selling* in regard to the girls was not of the *utmost quality* after all. He could not bear to have that sort of headline attached to his name. Especially not after the way that he had advertised for *them* so highly to his buyers.

Ezabella and Katalina could not stop feeling sad and hurt for Anni. Ever since she came back to the compound, the girls and everybody else would always see her talking to herself.

Anni would have manic episodes almost every day. She was put in a room by herself until El Jefe knew what he would do with her. His guards were at her door 24/7 yet they let her enter and exit the room whenever.

At times, Anni would walk out of the room with no clothes on exposing herself with her collar bone protruding out of her body. El Jefe had *allowed* her to still have some interactions with the rest of the girls but that did not last for long.

Anni did not speak to any of them.

She always looked lost as if she did not know where she was or what had happened to her.

All of the girls had a dismal look on their faces whenever they would see Anni. It was horrifying to see her that way. They tried to speak with her to possibly bring back some of her consciousness but to no avail. Instead they all felt pity for her. Only to realize that, at that moment, what had happened to Anni could have happened to any of them too. And so, they hid that fear deep down and went on to leave Anni alone to herself.

Anni had rope marks on her wrist showing that she had been binded for an extremely long period. While Jefe was trying to figure out what to do with her, he basically let her roam the compound because he knew that even if she wandered away that she would not go far.

El Jefe did not necessarily want that type of morale at the compound. But, he cared little about the girls' esprit de corps, so he let Anni go back and forth about as she pleased.

He was not worried at all. No one had been successful at escaping the walls of his fortress.

So why would he care about the girls' feelings about the situation or to possibly want to run off?

El Jefe was not willing to lose Anni so easily. He tried everything to *salvage* her.

So madrè Sonia was assigned to Anni for a short while.

And then one day, Anni disappeared altogether where she was never seen again.

Katalina guessed that it probably was Jefe that had ended her torment sooner than later. But she never found out. The whole situation about Anni was hushed up quickly.

One afternoon, Ezabella saw madrè Sonia walk out of a room carrying away what had been some of Anni's clothes. She had seen how Sonia was more *tolerable* and *kinder* to Anni. That was when Ezabella intuitively realized that *madrè Sonia may just be their way out of this evil place....*

Sonia

Whenever Ezabella and Katalina would see madré Sonia, she would have a stoic face that showed no emotions. But she was a beautiful woman.

Katalina had noticed that she was blind in her left eye. Sonia did not wear an eye-patch. She was not afraid to openly show that scar for everyone to see as if she had won a battle and carried the lasting impression of her triumph on her face.

Katalina was hesitant to inquire about it. Therefore, she decided not to.

She wanted to get to know Sonia a bit more; to feel a sense of closeness with an adult figure since her parents. However, Ezabella had other plans in mind. She wanted to get close to Sonia for help.

So far Sonia had been the only one to show the girls some kind of sympathy despite her facial expression and her cold demeanor toward them.

Ezabella made it her mission to find out as much as she could about madrè Sonia.

When she saw Sonia around the compound Ezabella would catch up to her and offer to help her with chores and anything else that she was doing. That was only possible when El Jefe did not require Ezabella to be by his side. El Jefe was more *attentive* to Katalina. Ezabella knew that so she took advantage of it to concentrate on what mattered most at the time: Sonia and an escape plan.

Madrè Sonia had ignored Ezabella's attempts for small talk every time until *one day*; when she saw that El Jefe had assigned Ezabella to work at *the facility.*

A LONG TIME AGO: Sonia was once one of those young girls that El Jefe had selected to work at the warehouse on the other side of the compound. The facility had makeshift rooms and was well protected by two armed guards up front, two at the back and the remaining three were inside with the girls. Only the specific people that El Jefe had chosen had access to this place. The guards had only two jobs at the facility: to secure the drugs and to stand watch over the girls working. There was no fraternizing or entertainment happening of any kind. Everyone had a fixed post and the guards knew very well what the consequence would be for not listening to El Jefe's direct orders.

However, doing the same task over and over became redundant for *Anthonio*. He was one of the guards that worked inside to watch the girls while they would cut, weigh and put the drugs into bags. Hence his attention would easily drift onto the girls that were assigned to work there, specifically toward *Sonia*. The other guards were tempted too but they would not dare to go against El Jefe's orders.

El Jefe ruled with an iron fist.

Those guards had seen what he was capable of doing. Therefore, their focus was quickly redirected to their task.

But Anthonio could not stop salivating at the fresh tenderness of Sonia's young body. He would watch her with tempting eyes. He looked like he was waiting for the perfect time to get her alone. But that time would never come unless he thought to himself that he had to do something about it.

Finally, Anthonio gave in to his temptation and acted on it.

One afternoon, he ordered Sonia to come with him. She did not know what to expect. She felt confused by his request.

Nevertheless, she reluctantly followed him.

Before she knew it, Anthonio had violated her in the most vile way.

Everything happened so fast that Sonia was in disbelief.

She could barely compose herself when Anthonio ordered her to go back to work without saying a word to anyone about it. Her tears had to be dried showing no feelings about that brute's actions.

So she returned to her post with Anthonio by her side escorting her as if nothing had happened.

Since he had done it once and he had gotten away; Anthonio was tempted to do it again. And so, he took advantage of Sonia every time that he had the chance to. He just could not restrain himself.

This went on for days.

Every guard present at the facility knew what was going on but yet they never said anything; not even to warn Anthonio of the consequence that he would receive if El Jefe was to find out.

El Jefe did not mix business with pleasure. He was strict about his investments and did not take kindly to anyone interrupting or compromising his affairs. But Anthonio's desire was stronger than his fear for El Jefe at the time so he did not care.

The guards' silence was blatantly disgusting.

Sonia despised each and every single one of them.

But who would she complain to?

The rules that El Jefe had were to be followed and each of his men knew them very well. They had to focus solely on work and they were not to touch the girls for any reason other than to escort them to and from the facility back to their room once they were finished. If at any time, any of the guards were to break his rule El Jefe would not delay to discard and to replace them. El Jefe treated the men that worked for him exactly how he treated the women with whom he would have sexual encounters with, like trivial and insignificant beings that could be replaced at any moment, by anyone else who would be willing to put in the work and obey at once with no questions asked.

The violation lasted for days until one day Sonia refused to go with Anthonio to that back room where he normally took her.

Anthonio lost his cool. His narcissistic self and fragile ego did not take that rejection well.

He let his temper flare out.

After days of forcefully getting what he wanted, he felt *entitled* as if Sonia had belonged to him. So it was no surprise that when Sonia had finally mustered the courage to say no, even though she was afraid for her life, that he saw her refusal as the ultimate disrespect forgetting that all along Sonia was a victim and that *he was the perpetrator.*

Anthonio hit Sonia with one violent blow to the face.

Soon after, he realized that he had made a huge mistake.

Anthonio panicked.

He tried to come up with an explanation for what he had done to Sonia. He had to make it sound good for when El Jefe would ask him what had happened.

So he enlisted the help of the other guards to cover up his slip-up.

In the meantime, Sonia was brought to the lodging of the madrés so that they could tend to the injury.

Madrè Liliana asked Anthonio what happened?

What could Sonia have possibly done to merit such a blow to her face that visibly would leave her with a scar for life?

Madrè Liliana looked upon Sonia's eye trauma. Anthonio was the cause of it.

He could clearly see that she was deeply upset; thus, with authority he raised his voice and told madrè Liliana to take care of it right away

"¡cuídalo!"

Then, he turned around and walked out of the madrè's lodging.

ONE HOUR LATER: Anthonio lied to El Jefe.

He wanted to tell him that he had caught Sonia trying to steal the drugs. However Anthonio could not accuse Sonia of being a thief because that would also imply that he did not do his job of standing watch over the girls while they work. And plus, where would Sonia have hidden the drugs when the girls only wore light clothing while handling the product.

Anthonio thought about several alternate explanations. In the end, with the help that he had enlisted from the other guards, he decided to go with accusing Sonia of stealing the drugs.

El Jefe was convinced by Anthonio's well fabricated story. Therefore, he replaced Sonia with MarieBella who was just as *beautiful.*

Sonia was punished for stealing and sent to the *box*. But in her mind, her consequence was ten times better than what she had endured at the hands of Anthonio, where she was sexually abused on a daily basis by that vermin of a man.

Sonia felt a moment of delight despite this horrible situation and the suffering that she had been through.

However, it did not take long for El Jefe to realize that Anthonio had lied to him.

Ever since Sonia had been replaced with MarieBella, Anthonio now had his eyes set on her.

She was beautiful, Anthonio thought to himself.

He seemed to have a type and showed a particular interest in MarieBella too.

So Anthonio went for it and used the same M.O. as he had done with Sonia.

But this time, things were different.

MarieBella suspected right away that Anthonio was up to no good.

She fought back.

MarieBella scratched Anthonio's face. She left distinct fingernail marks on his right cheek. Anthonio tried to restrain her but she would not have it.

She slipped out of his hands.

MarieBella made a run for it back to where the rest of the girls were. He ran after her to stop her but he was too late.

MarieBella was frantic but she managed to tell the other girls what Anthonio had attempted to do to her. The other guards did not like what they had just heard because that meant that they were complicit which they had been all along. And, once El Jefe would find out, they would all have a serious problem on their hands. The guards recalled for a moment that with Sonia the whole incident had been kept somewhat *quiet*. Anthonio's mess then had not been exposed out into the open like this. So with the MarieBella situation they were on edge. They knew that nothing good would come out of it for *them* when El Jefe would know the truth.

Those guards had no loyalty to Anthonio. They did not want to have any part of it knowing that they could lose their life over his actions.

So Anthonio explained to them that *it was a misunderstanding and that he'll fix it.*

However, it was too late for that now.

They had a serious issue to deal with.

The girls did not want to work anymore.

They all bundled up with each other in a corner of the room and left the product untouched. The guards outside had heard the disturbance so they all went inside to see what it was all about leaving their post unattended.

El Jefe could have installed cameras inside and outside of the facility. But, he did not. In his mind, he was so sure that his reputation perceived him well. So he was not worried about anyone failing to comply with his orders. And if they did, he would soon know about it.

Meanwhile, Anthonio threatened MarieBella and the other girls to return to work immediately or else they would suffer a severe punishment if they did not.

But his warning was in vain.

They refused and stayed exactly where they were.

Then Javier, who stood by and clearly saw that his attempt had failed, pulled Anthonio to the side and told him that he needed to fix this quickly. There was no way that he and the other guards would cover for him *this time.*

Everyone had lost track of time. When finally one of the guards realized it, and informed the rest of them that the girls had to be taken back to their rooms, at that moment, what would they do?

The guards looked at each other nervously.

Anthonio said to Javier to take the girls back to their rooms just like usual and that he would stay behind to do the work himself with the other guards.

They did not like that idea at all.

But, there was not enough time for them to think about any other options without raising any suspicions. Therefore, they unwillingly agreed.

Anthonio knew that he could not tell El Jefe that same lie that he had used for Sonia. He had to cover for the interruption of the work that had occurred. So with the help of Ramirez and Soledad, they made sure to finish weighing and bagging the drugs without anyone else finding out about it that evening.

The girls were reluctant to return to work the next day.

When the guards arrived to pick them up, they resisted the idea of going to the facility to work as if nothing had happened. At the same time, El Jefe was nearby making his way to meet guests. He *noticed* that something was off about the girls' behavior but he made no inquiry about it. Instead, he ordered Javier to take them at once to the facility.

MarieBella saw Anthonio that day. She tried her hardest not to break down but she was unsuccessful. The flashback of the event came to her mind. Thus, she quickly went into a panic attack. The girls tried to comfort her but that did not work. The guards could not afford to have another episode where the girls would leave the work for them to do once again. Therefore, Ramirez told Anthonio to swap posts with Javier who was standing watch out front of the facility.

Anthonio got upset and was ready to fix up MarieBella too just like he had done to Sonia. Soledad and Ramirez quickly grabbed him by his arms and advised him to do otherwise.

The guards managed to control the situation that day but for how long?

MarieBella would visibly get upset every time that she saw Anthonio.

Finally, it was Friday morning and MarieBella was steadfast on her decision not to work that day.

So during mealtime, she begged madrè Liliana to allow her to stay at the lodge with them. She pretended to be sick and told her that she was coming down with a fever. Of course that was a lie but Liliana did not need to know that. Her job was to make sure that the girls were fit to do whatever it was that El Jefe wanted them to do.

Therefore, madrè Liliana agreed to let MarieBella stay.

The following day when MarieBella was sent back to her room, the other girls told her that they had noticed that Anthonio had not reported for duty at the facility yesterday and that was unlike him. None of the guards had mentioned anything about his absence.

They had worked their shift as usual.

MarieBella was pensive after hearing that information. She was worried that she would get in trouble not knowing what Anthonio possibly could have told El Jefe about her. But the other girls convinced her that she did not need to be concerned because if Anthonio had said something about her to El Jefe she would have known by now. El Jefe never delayed and was always swift to hand-down consequences when needed. So there was nothing else for

MarieBella to do than to patiently wait and to see what would happen next.

Hours later, that evening, El Jefe requested that all of the guards that worked at the facility meet with him. That was when they knew that something was going on. When they arrived, they found Anthonio tied up flat onto the table that was used to cut up the drugs.

El Jefe had enlisted the help of some of his other men to secure the facility while he handled this situation here with Anthonio, Ramirez, Soledad and Javier.

The other three guards that were assigned to the facility were there too but somehow did not look as worried as them.

El Jefe began to question Ramirez and looked upon him with a calm demeanor. Ramirez was unsure what to respond. ...should he lie or tell his version of what had happened?

His behavior indicated to El Jefe that whatever would come out of his mouth next would be a lie.

Nevertheless, El Jefe did not wait for a response because he did not need one as he already knew what had happened. So he gave a signal to one of the guards that he had brought with him.

And just like that Ramirez received a bullet in the back of his head right where he stood. Soledad flinched as blood and brain particles flew on his face.

Javier did not wait to be asked that same question so he volunteered the answer right away.

El Jefe walked over to the table where Anthonio was tied up.

He picked up a pair of pruning shears. They looked sharp.

As he did so, El Jefe began to narrate to everyone present about Anthonio's story on why he was tied up on the table? Apparently he had attempted to skip town.

When Jefe's men finally caught up with Anthonio, his excuses for not showing up to work were that *he was not feeling well for duty that day; but, he also had a family emergency and thought that he could use a break from work altogether....*

El Jefe walked over to Javier and handed him over the gardening scissors. With a sneer, Jefe told Javier that it was time to cut off the bad weeds from the garden

"Creo que es hora de que cortemos las malas hierbas del jardín".

The sound of Anthonio's muffled voice was carrying on in the background as he was pleading for his life. El Jefe playfully tried to interpret what Anthonio could possibly say to him to have him spare his life. Whatever it was, Anthonio definitely swore to Jefe that he would never do what he did again.

"¡Lo juro, nunca lo volveré a hacer, por favor Jefe, por favor no me MATE!"

El Jefe's guards looked on and faithfully entertained his theatrics.

Jefe did not care about Anthonio's plea.

He did not torture Anthonio because he enjoyed it. That was not the way that he would reach gratification. His thing was torturing young girls. Instead, El Jefe did it because he had to make an example out of Anthonio for anybody else who would even think about disobeying him.

That night, Anthonio, Ramirez and Javier died.

Only Soledad was spared his life.

El Jefe had grabbed his gun ready to shoot Soledad but he second guessed himself once he heard himself say Soledad's name aloud.

As a young boy, he never liked his given name: *Soledad*. He thought that his name should be attributed to girls only and not to boys. Ironically, years later, Soledad's name was *solely* the reason why El Jefe had spared his life. Since the name Soledad was associated with the Virgin Mary and El Jefe thought of himself as a man of God, he refused to kill him.

Jefe believed that if he had done so that would have meant that he also would have killed *Mary* the mother of God committing the ultimate trespass against God himself. Therefore, this act would have resulted in serious repercussions in his life.

Lucky for Soledad, El Jefe was a *religious* man.

So instead, he had his men tie up Soledad and blindfolded him. Once done, they put him in a van and they drove off with him far away to somewhere remote and left him there where he was never to be seen again.

Sonia found out days later what had happened to Anthonio. She accidentally eavesdropped on the guards as they were making their way back to the facility.

El Jefe had cut off Anthonio's tongue and every single one of his fingers before he slit his throat. He had asked Javier to do it; but he did not have the stomach for it. Thus El Jefe violently stabbed him with the pruning shears in his neck and let him bleed out to death. Next, Jefe made Soledad disappear for good.

El Jefe wanted *total* obedience at all times and he must have it! That was the way.

Anybody that did not fall in line with his will paid the price for disobedience with either their life or suffered greatly. Hence, Sonia had finally gotten some peace of mind knowing that Anthonio and his accomplices had suffered just like she did and received their just due.

Thereafter, nobody thought anything else about Anthonio, Ramirez, Javier and Soledad since they vanished as they were soon replaced with other R.I.D.S of the world.

Ezabella's time at the facility was short-lived. It was as if El Jefe had vividly remembered what had happened with Sonia and MarieBella when they had worked there.

Thus, he decided not to let Ezabella: one of his *precious girls,* be among animals that would attempt to *ruin* her before *he* gets the chance to.

Sonia was *now* an ally.

The only thing that Ezabella was missing was an escape plan.

The both of them would have to work very hard at keeping their new found relationship a secret. But Ezabella was all in. She also knew that at some point she would have to make great efforts at building trust between her and Sonia otherwise this allyship would not last for long. Sonia was quick to notice things even with one eye remaining and the last thing that she wanted was for El Jefe to suspect that she was consorting with Ezabella. Just the mere notion that something was going on between the two, El Jefe would waste no time to make Sonia permanently blind and to perhaps crucify both of them at the stake. Sonia had seen him do something similar before; therefore, she was no stranger to his gruesome tactics that he would use to punish someone.

That evening, Ezabella found Katalina in bed rather early, crying incessantly with tears stains on the pillow. She knew that her little sister would not be able to hold on for too long in that place. She did tell Katalina the good news about her and Sonia's new forged bond.

But, Katalina did not seem to be reassured.

Ezabella knew that it was time for that escape plan to happen sooner rather than later.

The Escape

Ezabella woke up one morning with her father on her mind. She wondered where he was and most importantly was he looking for her? She definitely did not feel the same resentment toward her dad as she did for her mom. Those sentiments were different for each of her parents. Ezabella reflected on her relationship with her dad as a young child. Her feelings for him were still strong even though she knew that he had arranged a marriage for her.

She could not rationalize the reason as to why he would do that; however, she knew that he would never have let her marry someone not worthy of her. Her mom crossed her mind too; but she dismissed the thought of her quickly hoping that she was fine wherever she was. Her mother's actions were the reasons why she was here at the compound and desperately was looking for an exit plan out of this hell hole.

Katalina saw her in deep thought and decided to call her name aloud to get her attention. Ezabella heard her and shook her head quickly to rid the thoughts of her parents all together out of her mind. Every question that she wanted to ask them both would have to wait until one day when she would be reunited with them. Thinking about her parents at this time was a distraction; one that she could not let get in the way of what she needed to do.

Ezabella tried to talk to Sonia as many times as possible ever since they had connected. But prior to Ezabella, Sonia was careful not to speak to anyone. She kept to herself most of the time. Sonia would do her chores at the compound and obey all of the commands and requests that the men were giving her at any given time.

Of course their demands could not have been anything sexual because all of them even the new guards knew the story behind the scar that she had. And plus, it was clear to them that Sonia would be ready to put up a fight without a doubt if they would even show any signs of disrespect toward her.

Sonia had been living at the compound for some years now. She was well aware of the routines of the place. Especially the guards' shift change, their positions, their status and posts that they held and the most important information of them all, their *weaknesses*. It was Ezabella's job now to learn them as well. Her and Katalina definitely did not want to be the next ones to be stuck at the compound forever. They were grateful for Sonia's help but wondered why she never escaped after all of these years.

Ezabella was sure that some of the women, if not all of them had thought about escaping at some point…. *they had to*, she told herself.

Nevertheless, Sonia had agreed to help Ezabella and Katalina because she felt compassion for both of them. In her eyes they were innocent young girls who still had a chance to be spared living a painful and miserable life.

The escape plan that Sonia was willing to share with Ezabella was meant to be for *herself.* One that she always had wanted to use but never did because of fear.

Sonia had some doubts at first about trusting Ezabella and Katalina. After all, they are El Jefe' *prize girls* and knowing that information, she knew that he surely will not part from them so easily. But Sonia realized as well that Ezabella and Katalina had endured just as much pain as she had once upon a time at the hands of El Jefe.

Sonia knew that Ezabella had worked at the facility just like she did. So she decided to test her out. Sonia could not afford to *trust* her just like that. She wanted to see how far Ezabella was willing to go? And if she was really genuine about running away?

Sonia told Ezabella that she and Katalina would need money in order for the escape plan to work. And, the only way that they could get it was by stealing some of El Jefe's drug money.

Sonia told Ezabella that once she did that then she would be able to secure transportation for both of them to leave. Of course, Ezabella bought the whole story. She was not about to question Sonia. Ezabella knew that her and Katalina would need money if they were to be successful with the plan.

Ezabella did think that what Sonia had suggested to her was a big risk to take. Unfortunately, she did not have any other options. If that plan was going to get her and Katalina out of there then she would do it.

Ezabella began to plan out how she would make this *absolutely reckless idea* work.... Sonia knew that what she was asking Ezabella to do was dangerous. But, that was the only way that she could know for certain that Ezabella was not phishing for information to bring back to El Jefe.

Ezabella did not waste any time carrying out her plan to steal El Jefe's drug money.

Indeed, she had managed to steal a small amount of money at the facility. Sonia had told Ezabella to make her move *only* when *Alejandro* was assigned to work there on specific days. Alejandro was the only way that Ezabella would be able to get away with it. Any other guards would have made it impossible for Ezabella to enter the facility, let alone steal from El Jefe without being caught.

That same night, Ezabella found Sonia and gave her the money that she had stolen. She knew that she could not have held onto it for long. Especially not when madré Liliana would mostly be around to keep close watch on the girls despite the fact that the guards were there for that purpose.

Sonia thought that for a young girl, *Ezabella sure had a whole lot of guts to pull this off.*

She took the money from Ezabella and told her to wait until she reached out to her next.

She wanted to establish some distance between her and Ezabella so that no one began to suspect that she was plotting and consorting with the girls. In addition, Sonia needed to return that money to Alejandro as soon as possible, so that he could put it right back where it belonged without raising any suspicions from the other guards.

After one week, Sonia saw Ezabella in passing and instructed her to pretend that she was sick so that she could be sent to the madrés' lodge where she would be able to speak with her freely once they were there alone.

Sonia told Ezabella to watch out for when madré Liliana would be out of the lodge to go on food errands.

Ezabella did not have to worry about the other madrés because they would be too busy with incoming girls that El Jefe and his men had kidnapped and brought over to the compound during that late afternoon.

The time arrived and finally Ezabella saw madré Liliana leave. She quickly made her way to the lodge. She entered and saw that Sonia was already there waiting for her. They had to make this meeting very short. So Sonia promptly explained all of the details of the plan to Ezabella.

The truck that El Jefe used to bring in the drugs inside of the compound will be the way out for Ezabella and Katalina. Once the guards unload the products from the truck at the facility, they would feel more relaxed and at ease. Therefore, it would be easy for anyone to sneak onto the truck. Sonia had spent a lot of time observing the guards' routine. So she knew that this was a good way for Ezabella and Katalina to quickly get onto one of those trucks before the driver took off to return to the boat port without anyone noticing anything.

Madré Liliana would always think to herself that *El Jefe was not a man of much common sense*. Instead, he was so full of himself and very confident about his status as *El Jefe* that he rarely preoccupied himself with changing his patterns. This failure on his part to do so worked out perfectly for Ezabella's escape plan.

So there she decided with Sonia that on one early evening when the truck would be ready to leave the compound again, she and Katalina would make their move to get on. And once the driver would have reached his destination at the port and stop, they would get off unnoticed and make their way to find the boat that Sonia told them would be there waiting to leave exactly on time not one second late.

And this was the escape plan.

The whole plan itself was easy enough Ezabella thought.... But, Sonia quickly cautioned her not to underestimate how hard it would be to do all of that and to deceive everyone without being caught. El Jefe most of the time wanted Katalina and Ezabella by his side. But when he was occupied with other things and did not have the girls next to him, his men or and madré Liliana were certainly not too far away somewhere near to keep an eye on them.

Ezabella had listened attentively while Sonia was given her all of the particulars of the plan. She wanted to ask

Sonia what a boat looked like because she had never seen one before. But Ezabella chose not to. She felt that now was not the time to ask silly questions about something that Katalina probably would know and if not then they would figure it out together once there.

Sonia took a look at Ezabella and saw that she began to worry. So to ease her anxiety she offered to explain how she had come up with this plan.

After everything that had happened to Sonia at the compound at the hands of Anthonio and El Jefe, one night while she was all alone in one of the rooms at the lodge Sonia made an attempt to end her life. She thought at the time that she could not go on anymore. So she drank the poisoned tea that she had made for herself and she went to lay down knowing for sure that that night at the compound was going to be her last.

But Sonia woke up the next morning.

She was shocked.

The poisonous herbs that she had gotten from *Marcelo,* who she had met when she went on a food errand did not do what it was supposed to do.

So she went back to him when the next food errand occasion came around. Marcelo saw Sonia and looked delighted but she was not so pleased with him herself.

Sonia did not know it at the time but Marcelo owned a boat at the port. He was an older man and it appeared that he did not have any family because Sonia would always see him alone when she would go to the local market.

Marcelo had purposely given Sonia something other than what she had asked him because instead he wanted to offer her something better: *a way out.*

Whatever that Sonia was going through, he wanted her to know that she had options that would not require her to take her own life.

At the time, that encounter with Marcelo was the first and only one in a long time where Sonia had experienced someone who had shown her some *sympathy.*

So he told her that afternoon that whenever she would be ready, she could find him at the port on a specific day and time where he would unanchor his boat to sail somewhere far away. He never told her where that place was and she did not care to know. All that Sonia needed was to one day build the strength and courage to take on Marcelo's offer to sail aboard the *Sunflower.*

THAT DAY FINALLY CAME: Ezabella and Katalina had not slept for two days now. Their anxieties were heavy on their hearts.

In addition, as of late, they had noticed that El Jefe peculiarly would give them things to do *separately.* Ezabella thought that it was as if Jefe had suspected that the two of them were plotting something. And, he wanted to make sure that whatever it was that they were doing that it would not come to pass. But little did he know that Ezabella and

Katalina's escape plan with the help of Sonia was already put into motion….

That evening *almost* everything had worked according to plan just like Ezabella, Sonia and Katalina had talked about and rehearsed for days. With the exception of *one thing*.

Ezabella never made it onto the truck with Katalina.

Instead, she *sacrificed* herself so that Katalina, her little sister, could escape.

When Ezabella got caught and was brought back to the compound everything changed for *Sonia*. Her heart sank and her *own* escape plan with Alejandro was in jeopardy.

That night of the escape, the whole compound went into high alert.

El Jefe had stepped away momentarily to go into town for some business.

As soon as he came back, his men informed him of what had occurred and that the only one that they were able to catch was Ezabella.

El Jefe went *wild*.

He went full blown on a *manhunt*.

He immediately asked his men to bring Ezabella to him.

Upon seeing her, with rage, he reached and grabbed her neck and started to squeeze it with both hands. He screamed at Ezabella and demanded that she tell him where Katalina was. Ezabella was not about to say anything to him. She would much rather die than to tell him what she knew.

In the meantime, Sonia was pacing back and forth worrying to death. Alejandro told her that it was no use to do so and that they could not worry about Ezabella anymore because it was out of their hands. Sonia thought so too; therefore, she refocused her attention about finding out if Katalina had made it onto the Sunflower.

She needed to know what had happened to her for sure, so she asked Alejandro to inquire about her diligently. Alejandro agreed and went to speak to the other guards to find out more information. He returned and told Sonia that it seemed as though they hadn't found Katalina as of yet. Sonia blew out a deep breath.

She was half pleased with that news because she knew that now El jefe would certainly pry it out of Ezabella by any means necessary.

Sonia did not know how long it would take for El Jefe to get all of the information that he needed from her? Ezabella was a strong girl Sonia thought but she did not know how long Ezabella would last before she said anything to El Jefe about the escape plan or her.

Sonia did not say anything to Alejandro about it but in her mind, she knew that she had to free Ezabella. Alejandro looked at Sonia and sensed that she was thinking about some way to help Ezabella and he made his feelings about that idea known.

Alejandro was strongly against it.

He had fallen in love with Sonia.

All that he wanted to do was to escape with her.

For the short time that Alejandro had worked for El Jefe, he already knew that Jefe would employ all means and do whatever was necessary to find Katalina; therefore, if Sonia were to help Ezabella escape all four of them would feel the full wrath of El Jefe. There would be no place to hide for any of them.

They would have to be on the run and Alejandro was not willing to abandon his own plans for Ezabella.

Sonia knew that she would be asking Alejandro for too much if he were to help her with her plan to free Ezabella. Sonia couldn't help but to feel guilty about Ezabella getting caught escaping from the compound. Therefore, she worked on a solution to her problem on her own praying that Ezabella and her would make it out of the compound alive soon enough.

Meanwhile, El Jefe searched heaven and earth for Katalina. He was adamant and relentless to find her ever since she had successfully escaped his fortress.

Decision

Everything was set for Sonia and Alejandro to escape.

But Sonia heard that El Jefe had called upon the *good doctor* to come up to the compound so that he could get Ezabella to talk.

Sonia had to think about something quick.

Days had passed since Katalina had escaped. During that time, Sonia had purposely led Alejandro to believe that she had given up on saving Ezabella.

But that was not true of course.

Sonia prayed to God for a sign. She was waiting for divine intervention and anything that would indicate to her how to free Ezabella.

It was difficult to move freely around the compound. Sonia thought of every possible way that she would be able to get Ezabella out of there. But first she needed to speak with her.

Jefe had Ezabella held up in the *box* room under heavy security. Sonia knew that El Jefe was too busy looking for Katalina. So, one afternoon, she took advantage of that fact and went to speak to the guards and convinced them to let her see Ezabella.

Upon seeing her, Sonia's eyes teared up. Ezabella was not in a good shape. El Jefe had let his men rough her up. Ezabella was no longer El Jefe's *prize girl*. Instead, he despised her and it was obvious to Sonia that Ezabella's days were numbered.

In the meanwhile, Alejandro was part of the search party that had gone to the port with El Jefe to search for Katalina.

El Jefe had his men search every boat and questioned everyone on sight at the port.

But nothing came up. No one knew or had seen anything out of the ordinary.

El Jefe was enraged. So he decided to have a couple of his men stationed at the port as lookouts. Jefe thought to himself that *there was no way that Katalina had just disappeared like that... someone at the port must have helped her....*

Alejandro tried his best to unsuspiciously steer away El Jefe's men from discovering that Marcelo's boat was one of the boats that had not come back to the port as of yet.

That evening, when he returned to the compound, Alejandro found Sonia and urged her to move forward with their plan to leave as soon as possible. He did not show it; but Alejandro was worried about El Jefe finding out that Sonia had helped Katalina escape.

Sonia cared about Alejandro.

After everything that had happened to her, she thought that she would never be able to care and to trust someone again. But Alejandro changed her heart. She definitely felt a sense of attachment toward him; but she was not willing to give up on saving Ezabella.

One early morning, Sonia found out from Alejandro that the *good doctor* will be in town in the next two days.

Sonia felt terrified. She still had not come up with a plan to free Ezabella. At this point, Sonia wanted to give up hope. She thought to herself that maybe just maybe Alejandro might have been right all along about Ezabella's current situation. That it was out of their control and that there was nothing else that they could do about it now. After all, Sonia had done everything that she could for Katalina and Ezabella. She was not responsible for them anymore. But her conscience was weighing heavy on her. It was strongly imposing on her to do the right thing. Ezabella needed her help once more.

Sonia had one more day to figure out what she was going to do to free Ezabella. The pressure became too much for her. She asked Alejandro one more time to please reconsider helping her. But his answer remained the same. He insisted that it was best that she let it go and that she concentrated on their own plan and future out of the compound. Alejandro had worked out everything for the two of them to leave. There was no way that he was going to compromise his plan to free Ezabella. Sonia could not stop to think about how selfish Alejandro was, but deep down she felt that he was right. She was running out of time and still had not come up with any getaway plan. So, Sonia finally conceded to Alejandro. She could not resist anymore and accepted defeat. The obstacle was too great. In addition, Sonia had a secret that she had been holding on to for a while now. Thus, this time around she had more to lose if she was to get caught helping Ezabella to escape.

THAT DAY FINALLY CAME: The *good doctor* was due to arrive at any moment during the day. Sonia felt sick to her stomach but she went along with Alejandro's plan. She carried on with her chores for the day and acted as usual. Later on, she returned to the lodge and heard that two other madrés were trying to decide who would go on a food errand for that day. Sonia knew that only herself and Liliana were to leave the compound ever since the escape per El Jefe's orders. Yet the two women were conflicted about who would go as if Sonia was unavailable.

So she asked one of the madrés, where Liliana was? One of them replied that she was not feeling well to go this time. Suddenly, the light at the end of the tunnel that Sonia was desperately waiting for appeared. At that moment, she realized that this news was an opportunity that she needed to seize right away. Sonia recalled that ever since she had been at the compound, Liliana had never been sick. Liliana was one of those ancient women that was as strong as a bull in every aspect. So, Sonia coolly told the two madrés that stood in front of her that she would go. At last, she had recovered all hopes. But, she had to move fast.

Sonia said not one word of this to Alejandro.

She stepped out of the lodge and walked around to the back to see if the van that they would normally use to go on food errands was there. She inspected it and noticed that the keys were there. Next, she quickly made her way to where Ezabella was held up. She did not know what she would say to the guards this time but she figured that it would come to her then. She arrived and noticed that the same guards that she had talked to before were there. Sonia demanded to see Ezabella. They gave her a look and questioned her presence there. At that moment, she used her authority as a madré just like she had seen Liliana do so many times to explain to the guards that she needed to get Ezabella ready for the *good doctor* once he would arrive. The guards were not convinced and El Jefe was not there to confirm. He was still busy looking incessantly for Katalina. They asked her to leave as they were not informed that she would come to get Ezabella. Then, Sonia came up with a different approach. She appealed to the guards' fears of El Jefe to persuade them to let her in. They hesitated momentarily then agreed. Sonia entered the room and saw that Ezabella was barely conscious. She swiftly removed the ropes on her wrist and forced her to stand up. Ezabella was weak and in pain. Sonia told her to find the strength to walk because *this* was the escape. They had to go now. As Sonia exited the box room with Ezabella, the guards grudgingly escorted them to the lodge. They told her to hurry up. Once inside, Sonia rushed to get to the exit door at the back of the lodge where the van was parked. But, she was interrupted in her steps by the two other madrés that she had spoken to earlier. They were inquisitive. The last thing that she wanted was for Liliana to come out of her room if she was to hear all of this talk in the hallway. Once again, Sonia used her authority to firmly end all questions from the two women. They followed Sonia with their eyes as she made her way to one of the rooms nearby. They then, reluctantly returned to their chores. Sonia waited for them to be out of sight and moved on quickly to the back door. Finally, she reached the van. She instructed Ezabella to stay put and well hidden under the drapes that covered the crates that were in the van. Ezabella nodded. Sonia rushed to get into the van and turned on the ignition. She tried to control her nerves. But that was just impossible at the time. Too much was at stake. She knew that it would not take long for the guards to suspect that something was going on once too much time would have elapsed. Sonia swiftly drove up to the gate and was stopped by one of the guards. He began to question her. She answered every single one of his questions. But he was still not satisfied. So, he proceeded to ask the other guard to go out back to the van to check it out. At that moment, Sonia knew that if that guard was to search the van it would be over for her and Ezabella. Her foot was ready to press down on the gas pedal as a last resort and attempt to make it out of the compound. And, then, she heard a familiar voice that called out to the other guard as he was about to open the back door of the van. That voice said that it was okay to let her go since El Jefe had given orders that she and Liliana were the only ones allowed to leave the compound on food errands. Sonia looked in her driver side mirror and saw that it was Alejandro.

Sonia held her composure. The guard finally let her pass the gates.

She watched Alejandro slowly disappear out of her sight in the mirror. That moment was when they exchanged their last eye contact.

Alejandro had worked hard to set up a safe exit plan for them. He had made small deals here and there as fast as he could to come up with enough money to afford them transport out of the compound for good.

Sonia could have brought Ezabella to the rendez-vous that she had with Alejandro but she did not. It became clear to her that this encounter with Alejandro might have been the last time that she would ever see him again. She felt guilty about the way that she chose Ezabella over him but she knew that he would understand. She also knew that Alejandro would do everything in his power to buy her as much time as possible so that she could escape with Ezabella and reach her destination safely that he had previously set up for them.

Sonia had made her *decision.*

HOURS LATER: Sonia reached the checkpoint that would lead her to the border. During the whole drive, she kept on worrying about Alejandro. By now, the guards at the compound with Liliana and El Jefe knew that she was on the run too and that she had been the person that had helped Katalina escape. Sonia could only imagine the mayhem that was happening at the compound right about now. Nevertheless, she arrived at the border and paid for her way through and drove across. Shortly after, Sonia reached the place where Alejandro had set up everything for them. There she found a car. She quickly inspected the vehicle and found a firearm, some money, cans of food and clothes. She quickly helped Ezabella out of the back of the van and had her sit in the passenger side. She then resumed driving. As the car moved forward, and they got further and further away, Sonia and Ezabella seemed to have felt a sense of peace in the air. They stared at the open road in front of them showing this vast land ahead where they would now begin a new life, all *three* of them.

Boat Ride

Katalina had to move fast. She hardly could concentrate or remember the information that Sonia had given her. Her heart was racing. The port was busy and filled with people. Katalina could hear engines roaring, loud voices, noises that came from all over the port. She did not know how long she had before the boat would leave. She needed to get off the truck quickly. When the driver finally stopped the truck, she waited for him to open that door. At last, the wood crate box where she had been hidden inside made it off the truck. She peeped through the openings to see where it was being carried: inside of a cargo container. As soon as she felt that the crate was put down, and that the coast was clear she quickly came out of the crate and ran to assimilate into the crowd close by.

Katalina had to look for a boat that had a *Sunflower* emblem. That symbol meant that the boat would always depart at dawn marking the ending of twilight before sunrise. But most importantly to Katalina the Sunflower also meant the rise of a new day, where she would get the chance to start her life over somewhere new and far away.

But in the meantime, since it was already evening time, Katalina thought that it would be hard to find that boat out of so many at the port. To Katalina, all of those boats somewhat looked the same. Then, Katalina remembered that Sonia had told them that once there they would have to look for an old man of a dark complexion. But, it seemed that there were so many men that looked that way all over the port already. How would she find the one that Sonia had told her about? And, Katalina was unsure about how she would find that boat as well? She started to panic and tears came down her cheeks.

She stood in the middle of the crowd not knowing what to do. But then, she remembered that Sonia had told them that the boat would be docked at the other end of the port where women sold peanuts and served hot meals to passengers and crew members before departure. She made her way there fast but did not need to reach the end because as she was about to pass the boat in question, Katalina accidentally bumped into a lady and as she did so that was when she noticed *an old man* that appeared to be who Sonia had described to her. Katalina was not certain of it but she let her instincts guide her. The old man looked like he was preparing to depart. Katalina moved quickly toward the boat and at long last she saw the Sunflower symbol carved out on the side of the boat that she had been looking for.

She made her way onto the boat. Katalina had just made it on time.

THE FIRST NIGHT ON THE BOAT: Katalina had nightmares. She kept on replaying in her mind the night of the escape. They both ran side by side. Katalina recalled that she reached the truck and pulled on the latch and got on. Katalina had not noticed that Ezabella had stopped running. Katalina kept on asking herself what went wrong?

They had spent so much time rehearsing and thinking about every detail of that plan. Everything had gone according to their plan until at the last minute *something must have happened*, Katalina thought. During their escape, Ezabella quickly realized that one of them had to stay back if the plan was to continue to work. Katalina had not noticed anything because she was ahead of Ezabella running at that time. Katalina's heart was severed in thousands of pieces. She replayed the scene in her head over and over again when the guards caught Ezabella. They surrounded her. Their rifles pointed right in her face. At that moment, Katalina gasped for air. She was distraught and in disbelief that Ezabella was not next to her on that truck. Katalina could not stop thinking about what would happen to Ezabella? Her only friend and sister, what will she endure at the hands of El Jefe? Katalina knew that the torture would never end. El Jefe would make Ezabella pay for the both of them for attempting to escape. Katalina did not sleep well that night. She would fall asleep out of fatigue only to wake up crying after her nightmares. She cried so much that tears soaked the collar of her soiled t-shirt. Katalina was inconsolable. Ezabella had sacrificed herself to give Katalina time to escape. Katalina *just* could not believe what had happened.

Katalina felt that she had been on that boat for *days*; but really it only had been three days. She felt sea sick from sunrise to sunset. And, she did not know how long more she could take being on that boat?

All of the passengers aboard the Sunflower had been given a chance to start anew. Katalina found herself once again among strangers. She had no one to look out for her anymore, Ezabella was gone. However, there was a woman and her child that Katalina had noticed on the boat that reminded her so much of a time when she was with her parents. She longed for that moment where one day she would be reunited with her mother and father. That woman had been observing Katalina and felt sorry for her. She saw for herself that Katalina was traveling all alone. And, she just could not imagine how hard it was for a child to be all alone traveling on a long journey to somewhere unknown. So, the woman approached Katalina to give her something. She gently grabbed Katalina's hand and gave her what looked like a small round rock. But in reality, the rock was a type of dry fruit called *ochre*. The woman told Katalina to put the rock in her mouth and to hold it under her tongue. The saliva in Katalina's mouth would dissolve the rock slowly where the bitter substance of the rock would end her nausea.

After a couple of minutes, Katalina felt better. She was grateful to the woman for this.

Katalina still could not fall asleep. Since her nausea had passed, Katalina felt free to go on the deck. She found *the old man,* Marcelo, navigating his vessel peacefully. Katalina looked at the vast ocean and the horizon. She realized then that she had been so far away from home and had no idea of when she would return. Katalina took a look at Marcelo. She wanted to ask him where they were going? But on second thought, she figured that she would not. In reality knowing where she was going was not going to help her feel better. Katalina was tired of running and she was heartbroken. Katalina had no idea how long this journey across to a new land would take her but she did not care. She felt this burning pain in her chest every time her mind thought about Ezabella. Despite the fact that she felt guilty about feeling this way, Katalina had a strong desire to be away from everything and everyone that had caused her pain. Even if it meant that she would leave behind all of the people that she loved. She thought about it over and over again but what could she have done differently? If she had, she too would have been caught.

Katalina snapped out of her unhappy mood. She caught a glimpse of Marcelo and recalled the way that he had abruptly stopped her and frowned his eyebrows at her on the deck to ask her where she was going? And where were her parents? What was she doing on his boat? It was not until Katalina mentioned Sonia's name that Marcelo stopped to question her. He then rushed her to find her way underneath the deck of the boat before he let the rope of the anchor loose and rapidly steered his boat off the dock.

Wandering

Finally, the Sunflower had reached its destination. After Marcelo tied the anchor to his boat, he rapidly made his way below deck. He told all of *them* that they had to go fast before the Marine Port Custom Brokers would come to inspect his boat for import of goods. Marcelo did not even get to finish his sentence when everyone began to leave. It was as if they already knew what to do. They scattered among the crowd on the dock and all of the passengers that Katalina was on the boat with had disappeared out of sight. Katalina was scared and had nowhere to go. So the one thing left for her to do was to follow that woman with her small child off the boat. The woman saw that Katalina was walking behind her. She did not fuss about it, instead she motioned her to move quickly. Moments later, Katalina found herself standing in front of a white van where the rest of the passengers that she thought had long been gone were there too. Her facial expression was puzzled and the woman had noticed, so she looked at Katalina with reassurance that she needed to get on that van with them *too*. They all arrived at an undescribed location. They were dropped off and one by one they entered the premises. There, Katalina found food and water. She sat down on a cot and watched as everyone else was eating. No one said anything. It was weird, Katalina thought. Everyone already knew what to do except for her. She asked herself, how could that be? But she did not want to think about that too much. Katalina was exhausted. She slowly fell asleep without her realizing it. She woke up hours later to the sight of an *almost* empty space. Everybody had left except for that woman and her child. For some reason, that woman took pity on Katalina and just could not leave her by herself. So she stayed back for the next *pick up*. Finally a van came to their location. They all got on and the driver drove away. When they arrived at the next place, Katalina noticed that it was a restaurant. But instead of entering through the front door, they were ushered to the back where they went down some stairs into a basement. Katalina was uncomfortable in this new environment. Once again, she found herself in a place where she did not like the idea of not being able to move about freely. She spent the first week or two in the basement working on little chores. The woman would leave her small child with Katalina while she would be called upstairs to *help out.* Whatever that it was that the owners of the restaurant had her do she surely did not like it. She was always so tired and had an unpleasant odor about her whenever she returned to the basement. Katalina did not want to complain to the woman about anything because at least she had a roof over her head and food to eat, but she asked herself at what cost?

One day, Katalina woke up to find herself alone in that basement. The woman and her child were gone. She was all alone once *again.* A small-built man came down to get her and spoke to her in a language that she did not understand. That man looked fairly young and was maybe in his twenties. Katalina felt forced to follow him upstairs.

She immediately met the owners of the restaurant. It was a woman and her two sons. One looked so mean and rough. The other one was *kinder* to Katalina. But the way that he was nice to her quickly reminded Katalina of El Jefe. And surely that same day, he showed his true colors. Katalina heard the woman shout to him "Vincent, leave her alone. I don't wanna deal with your shenanigans again. She DON'T want you! LEAVE her!". Of course, Katalina had no idea what that woman had just said but she had a feeling that it was not safe anymore for her to stay there with these people.

Katalina thought about the woman and the child from the boat. She tried to come up with her own explanation as to why maybe the woman had abandoned her here. She figured in her mind that it probably was too much of a responsibility to take care and to feed *two children* at the same time. Katalina did not want to dwell on the idea for too long, but she was *hurt*.

Vincent would not let loose. He started to make Katalina feel really uncomfortable. He would do things such as intentionally leaving the door of the bathroom open so that while Katalina was occupied with chores and she would pass by, she could see *everything explicitly hang...* She concluded that Vincent would make every attempt to lure her to him. Katalina was disgusted. On another occasion, he gently brushed her with his body and landed behind her back. Katalina froze as she quickly had a flashback of a past experience with El Jefe. Vincent put both of his hands, one on each side of her waist and rubbed his genitalia on her. Katalina's body jerked, she turned around and slapped him real good on his cheek. Vincent was astonished. He did not expect such a reaction from Katalina. Before this, he had looked at her as if she was a fragile lamb needing attention. Vincent quickly ran upstairs to his *mama*. She saw the red mark on her son's cheek. She stormed downstairs to the basement and in exchange returned that slap to Katalina. Vincent was there to witness the whole thing. He tried to calm his mother down but instead she furiously cussed out Katalina. And lastly as she regained her cool, she looked at Katalina and said to her "**if** you don't do what my son wants you to do then you can't STAY here". Katalina stood there not understanding a word of what that woman said to her. She wanted to run then but Vincent and his mother were blocking the way up to that basement door. Katalina realized that she could not remain there any longer. So the next day, when Vincent came to get Katalina, she knew that that was her moment to just run out the front door and to never come back to this place again. Katalina had nowhere to go but at least, she was now free to wander the streets.

Jaymes

Katalina's entire life changed after she met Jaymes.

Jaymes was handsome. He was timid but confident about himself.

He rarely was seen with friends but he had them.

He had a job and he lived alone.

Jaymes was in college completing his undergraduate degree. He was very good with his hands. He aspired to be an engineer. Jaymes minded his business and mostly stayed to himself. But that changed once he met Katalina.

One day, Jaymes had left work and he was on his way back home. He took a shortcut as opposed to his usual route. That was when someone caught his attention from the sidewalk. So he pulled up his car to the curb. He got out of his car to walk toward the person that he had seen while driving. That someone was *Katalina.*

He did not know it then but Katalina had been lingering in the neighborhood for some time now. Katalina was in bad shape. She had no money and she did not speak the language of this land. Katalina had no idea where she was or where she was going. At some point, she had felt safe and secure when she stayed with the woman and her child that she had met on the boat. But her time at that restaurant did not last long; she had to leave. Katalina had nowhere to go. But still, in her mind, nowhere to go was much better than staying somewhere where she would be taken advantage of. Katalina recalled her mother's last words to her " that in times of need call upon the spirits to help guide you…". Katalina had been sleeping in bushes of residential areas, in parking lots of retail stores and in parks. So far this way had worked for her but that was not what she was accustomed to of course. In addition, Katalina was hungry. She knew where to go to find *scraps* of food. And, if she was lucky enough on those evenings, an *untouched* meal would be waiting for her. Even though they could have gotten in trouble for it, some of the servers at those restaurants would manage to help Katalina in small ways with food. Katalina had learned after her experience with Vincent at his mom's restaurant that the people that lived here wasted a lot of food that could have easily fed a couple of families back in her village, she thought.

Katalina was in desperate need of a shower. She would go to the public restrooms at those retail stores and somewhat do a *wash- up*. On one occasion her menstrual cycle had come. She recalled taking a roll of toilet paper with her as she exited the restroom…

So far she had been pretty good at figuring out her new environment; but Katalina was just too tired. She did not know how long she would be able to survive like this. Something had to give. So she would talk to the sun at sunrise and talk to the moon after sunset and smile at the blue sky despite her circumstance hoping that her current situation would change soon.

Jaymes appeared in her life at the right moment.

Jaymes had a feeling that Katalina may not be from here. He approached her and introduced himself to her but he quickly realized that she did not understand his language. Nevertheless, he tried his best to express to her that he wanted to help her. He made some universal hand gesture to indicate to her that he would buy her food if she wanted something to eat. Katalina understood what he tried to say to her by his hand movements. She stared at him and took a good look at him from head to toe. Jaymes was a young man but he was still too old for Katalina, she could tell that there was a distinct difference in age between them. She also noticed that he was easy on the eyes. But the last thing that she needed was to be baited by a man's charm, good looks and some food to end up once more in a situation where she would be kept captive. Jaymes did not quite understand the reason for her stare but he figured that was her way to determine if it was safe for her to follow him. When he realized that she was undecided as to what to do. He simply told her to wait for him. Then he turned around and walked away. After he left, Katalina thought about it again and wondered if she had made a mistake by not following him. She could not worry about it anymore. Katalina had endured so many obstacles at this point and Ezabella had sacrificed herself for her that she could not compromise her safety and her freedom.

Katalina started to walk when she heard Jaymes called out to her. He had bought a whole pizza pie. She was not sure what to make of it. Katalina might have been hungry but she was not about to accept food from a stranger where she could possibly be drugged and then taken. The smell of the pizza went through her nostrils and instantly her stomach growled. Jaymes heard it so he figured she needed some encouragement to eat. He took the first slice and ate it in front of her. As soon as he did that, Katalina grabbed two slices and ate them both simultaneously. Once she was done, Jaymes handed her the box with the rest of the pizza inside. She took it and walked away. He was a little surprised by her behavior but he made no fuss about it. Jaymes watched Katalina walk away not knowing if he would ever see her again. But he had a feeling deep down that he would.

Katalina was careful to make sure that he was not following her. She retreated to a spot that she had found in the park where she could sit in peace and eat the rest of the pizza for the night. She was grateful for the food. Jaymes had been another person graceful enough to care to give her food to eat.

That night Katalina thought about Jaymes and wondered if he was the *change* that she had hoped for. She looked at the moon and slowly fell asleep with the box of pizza in her hands.

Somehow for the next few days, Jaymes could not focus on anything else but his interaction with Katalina, however small it was. He wanted to see her again. On his way to work his eyes would search the streets for Katalina nonstop. Until one day, he spotted her by a small park where she had been spending her nights. He parked his car and walked over in her direction. He did not want to frighten her so he approached her slowly. Katalina, caught by surprise, was about to run when he told her "I have food, I know that you must be hungry". She still could not understand what he said to her but as soon as he did the hand gesture for "eating" she stopped in her tracks. The language that he spoke was new to her. Katalina only knew Haitian-Creole and Spanish. The native languages of her mama and papa. And Jaymes spoke to her in English. He showed her a bag that he held in his hands. It had fresh fruits in it. So she sat back down on the bench and he sat next to her and they just ate the fruits together.

Somehow for the next couple of days this was their interaction. He would find her at the park around the same time after his shift and would give her food to eat. It was hard for Katalina to trust anyone, especially after everything that she had gone through at the compound. But she was tired of sleeping in the bushes. Her clothes were dirty and she had not taken a shower in days. So she let herself be wooed by Jaymes slowly but surely after he had been kind to her all of this time. And that was how one day he convinced her to get into his car. This was a dangerous move. A leap of faith that Katalina took. She was all alone, with no family, she did not speak the language let alone knew exactly where she was. But she also knew that she would not be able to survive much longer on her own outhere in the streets.

Jaymes lived in the first floor apartment in a house. His neighbors watched him suspiciously as he said hi to them and quickly rushed Katalina inside the apartment. They made no fuss about it because they knew him to be reserved and a decent young man that would always pay his rent on time and went to school. Katalina was not afraid of him. Jaymes was not El Jefe or his men. By now Katalina was fifteen years old. She had spent two whole years at El Jefe's compound.

Ever since that day, Jaymes would go to work and come back home to find Katalina reading and learning English using his course work books and by watching television. Jaymes had bought Katalina more books and magazines for her to read.

He would leave her in his apartment and could not wait to come back to her in the evenings. When he was not home, he definitely did not want her to go out there. He thought to himself that it was selfish for him to think that way. Especially, when he had met Katalina on the streets where she had survived all of that time on her own. So instead, Jaymes made sure to make Katalina as comfortable as possible so that she would not leave.

Jaymes worked during the day and went to school in the evenings. After he finished class, he would come back home to her for dinner with all sorts of different delicious meals. Katalina had enjoyed all of them. That was the first time in a long time that she had a smile on her face.

During his spare time, Jaymes taught Katalina how to read, write and speak English and to cook. For the first three months that was their daily routine. Until one day, something more than she expected happened.

Katalina had never been with a man before.

She did not know how to feel about it after *it* happened.

Soon after, Katalina felt sick.

She would throw up all of her food.

She would complain of headaches that would turn into fever but quickly disappear.

Jaymes was not sure of what to do but he suspected that Katalina may be pregnant. Despite the fact that Katalina was still a novice in the English language, she knew that she needed to go see a doctor.

Jaymes knew that Katalina was all alone in the country. She had never mentioned to him having any family members here and she did not seem to have access to any identification documents. Jaymes was hesitant to take her to seek medical attention. She certainly was way younger than him. What would people say to him ? And how would he answer all of the questions that they would have for him in regards to Katalina? How could he explain it all?

Nevertheless, Jaymes searched for a planned parenthood clinic. Once he found one, he called first to ask questions before even going there. He would not risk raising suspicions.

So a couple of days later, Jaymes called out of work to take Katalina to the clinic. When they came back for the results, the doctor confirmed to them that Katalina was indeed expecting their first child.

Katalina had no idea what to do. She was just a child herself. Her English was still in the beginning stage. She had so many questions that she wanted to ask the doctor. She tried her best to ask them. And Jaymes did his best to translate what she wanted to ask.

In all of the conversations that Jaymes had with the doctor the only two words that Katalina managed to decipher were the words *abortion* and *adoption*. But the two words sounded the same to her. She had no idea what they meant, only that Jaymes had refused and flat out said *no* to both.

And since he was the only person at this time that she lived with and that had provided for her and given her a place where she felt mostly safe and at peace, she did not oppose his decision or anything that he had said to the doctor.

For the next several months, Katalina was feeling sick off and on, cranky and just nostalgic of her childhood memories of when she was with her mom and dad. Then, the thoughts of El Jefe would cross her mind at night when she would fall asleep only to wake up in sweat and tears. Jaymes would try to comfort her. But he did not understand her fears and extreme sense of panic that she would have at night when she would close her eyes. Only Katalina knew why. Now that she was expecting a child, El Jefe haunted her mind more and more. He had never left but this time it was worse. She kept on thinking that he would one day find out where she was. She could only imagine what he would do to her and her baby if he did.

Katalina had been with Jaymes for a whole year now. The planned parenthood clinic had been so good to them by providing Katalina and Jaymes with the medical care that Katalina needed herself and for their baby. To her knowledge, she gave birth to a healthy, handsome baby boy with a birthmark right by his navel that resembled the shape of a *tiny white spider* due to the hypopigmentation of his skin in that area.

Jaymes *somewhat* named his son after him.

After a couple of weeks, Katalina one night decided that the best thing that she could do was to leave her son with her father. The nightmares that she would have about El Jefe were too real for her. She felt that both of them would be in danger if she stayed.

Jaymes was no match for El Jefe and his men. He would not know how to protect them, she thought to herself. Katalina thought about telling Jaymes her story but she concluded that it would be best not to. She could only imagine what Jaymes' reaction would be. And she definitely did not want to be on the run with her baby or put them both in danger.

Katalina wanted to ask Jaymes to move but to where? Anywhere that they would go, El Jefe would have access to find them somehow and she did not want to compromise their safety.

Katalina was left once again not knowing what to do. She was still herself, just a teenager. She thought about what her mother would have said to her had she been there. Suddenly, she reminisced about the last moments that she had with her dad. She looked at her baby boy for the last time while he was in his bassinet peacefully sleeping. Then, she repeated over him the same last words that she remembered her dad had said to her. Next, she drew the sign of the cross over his forehead just like her mama had done for her. Lastly, she attached a tiger's eyes crystal necklace to the musical rattle toys that hung above his head in his bassinet.

**(Katalina had learnt a lot while with Jaymes. She had made it her business to learn as much as she could. Her comprehension in English had improved. Jaymes encouraged Katalina to speak English; while at the same time, he would never miss an opportunity to affectionately tease her about her accent. She had fallen in love with *crystals* while reading one of Jaymes' science books).

Ultimately, one night Katalina quietly got out of bed. And without making a sound she got dressed, grabbed a small bag to put what she thought that she would need. She took one more look at them both while they were peacefully sleeping, then she turned around, walked through that door and never came back. That was the most difficult decision that she had to make in her young life at the time. But, Katalina knew that as long as El Jefe was looking for her, she would not have a normal life. Jaymes and her baby would be in danger and she couldn't take that risk.

TWO MONTHS LATER: Jaymes relocated after he realized that it was unnecessary to continue searching for Katalina. She was not at her usual spots where she used to be. He knew that this time, he was not going to find her.

Been There Before (Alone)

Ever since that night, one year had passed and Katalina was back on the streets off and on all alone. Katalina would do small work for small change to find places to stay and food to eat. But everything was not the same anymore.

Katalina felt different because she was *different*.

Her life was unlike that of a typical teenager. She was hunted by El Jefe. She wondered if one day she would ever break free from him.

She had no idea what to do or where to go next?

She had no plans.

She knew that El Jefe would stop at nothing to find her…his prize *jewel*.

Whom could she trust?

She thought to herself all of these questions and the final one being… *kounye a kisa?*

Now what?

TO BE CONTINUED...

NEXT ON FIERCE BOOK SERIES:

Book II

FIΣRCΣ

———————

BECOMING

About the Author

You can find out more about the author by visiting their webpage and by following them on Facebook and Instagram by using the link and the QR code below.

www.séverinetheauthor.com

https://www.facebook.com/SeverineTheAuthor/

SEVERINETHEAUTHOR

Made in the USA
Middletown, DE
14 October 2023